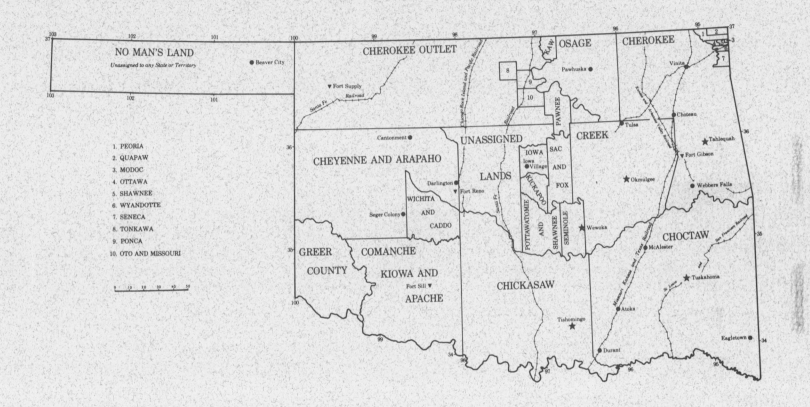

NO MAN'S LAND
Unassigned to any State or Territory

1. PEORIA
2. QUAPAW
3. MODOC
4. OTTAWA
5. SHAWNEE
6. WYANDOTTE
7. SENECA
8. TONKAWA
9. PONCA
10. OTO AND MISSOURI

INDIAN TERRITORY, 1866-1889

THE STATE OF
SEQUOYAH

Cattle drive, Osage County.

THE STATE OF SEQUOYAH

AN IMPRESSIONISTIC LOOK AT EASTERN OKLAHOMA

Text By
JERALD C. WALKER

Photography By
DAISY DECAZES

THE LOWELL PRESS / Kansas City

This volume is dedicated to James and Ann Linn.
Their suggestion launched this project and their
inspiration saw it to its conclusion.

Maps on endsheets from *Historical Atlas of Oklahoma,* Second Edition, Revised and Enlarged,
by John W. Morris, Charles R. Goins, and Edwin C. McReynolds.
Copyright © 1965, 1976 by the University of Oklahoma Press.

Library of Congress Cataloging in Publication Data
Walker, Jerald C.
The state of Sequoyah.

1. Oklahoma—History, Local.
2. Oklahoma—Description and travel—1981- .
I. Decazes, Daisy, 1955- .
II. Title.
F694.W35   1985   976.6'05   85-11362
ISBN 0-913504-95-5 (alk. paper)

Text Copyright © 1985 by Oklahoma City University

Photography Copyright © 1985 by Daisy Decazes

Printed in the United States of America by The Lowell Press

CONTENTS

Foreword vii

Between Two Worlds:

   An Oklahoma Perspective 1

The State of Sequoyah Convention . . 5

Indian Removal 9

The Indian Republics and Indian Territory 14

The New State 49

A Profound Change of Identity . . . 54

A Complex Area of Great Promise . . 71

Notes 105

ACKNOWLEDGMENTS

Special appreciation to James P. and Ann A. Linn and Robert S. Kerr, Jr., and Lou Kerr for their encouragement and support of this project. Thanks to Letha Deen Weeks, Professor Valor Thiessen, Susan McVey, Dr. Peter Denman, LaDonna Kramer Gooden, and Dr. Frank Pfaff, all members of the Oklahoma City University staff and faculty, for their assistance in preparing the manuscript. Daisy Decazes expresses special thanks to Sarah and George Scott, Joan Killingsworth Dreisker, the Reverend Richard M. House, the Honorable Ross Swimmer, the Reverend Stanley Warfield, Jim Stafford, Monte and Floyd Truman, Jim Ikard, Marty Jennings, Marilyn Myers, Mrs. Doug Whitehorn, and Sonny and Clayton Pratt for assistance during her travels through eastern Oklahoma. Special thanks to Dr. Carter Blue Clark for his thoughtful foreword. Finally, very special appreciation to Virginia, Elisabeth, and Anne Walker for their support and patience.

FOREWORD

The example of the Walker family in eastern Oklahoma is both informative and instructive. They reflect the pioneering experience of thousands of families who trekked into Oklahoma. Theirs is a part of the odyssey of families who ventured forth into a new land seeking not only their fortunes but also their destinies. Their journey brought them from east Tennessee to Indian Territory.

More than most Anglo immigrant families, the Walker family became acquainted with Indian people already present in eastern Oklahoma. At the same time the white frontier expanded, the Indian frontier receded. Members of the Walker family viewed both sides of the issue of encroachment. Jerald C. Walker's account offers an original glimpse of the philosophical and cultural mix of Indian and white in the area that was Indian Territory.

Growing to adulthood in the Punkin Center Community (only outsiders and those persons "putting on airs" called it Pumpkin Center), now a part of suburban Tulsa, Dr. Walker began his long involvement with the Methodist Indian people belonging to the historic and predominantly Creek Haikey Chapel Indian United Methodist Church. His mother's people were mixed-blood Cherokee Baptists.

Following his education at Oklahoma City University, the Divinity School of the University of Chicago, and the School of Theology at Claremont, California, Jerald Walker served on the staff of Temple United Methodist Church, San Francisco, and as Chaplain and Assistant Professor of Religion at Nebraska Wesleyan University. At the age of 29 years he became the nation's youngest college president as chief executive of Pershing College, Beatrice, Nebraska. He also served as vice president for university relations at Southwestern

University, Georgetown, Texas, and as president of Baker University, Baldwin City, Kansas, before returning to his undergraduate alma mater, Oklahoma City University as its thirteenth president.

Dr. Walker's experience as a native son of eastern Oklahoma, historical study, and observations combine to offer unique insight into the background and life of eastern Oklahoma. Growing up on the boundary of the two worlds, Indian and white, his background afforded him a dual heritage. He provides in this volume an impressive survey of a significant number of the milestones in the development of Indian Territory and the State of Oklahoma.

Daisy Decazes, a native of France, is a much respected photographer. This is her second photographic essay on Oklahoma. Her first book, *Western Oklahoma,* was well received. That effort was done in cooperation with Dr. William Banowsky, then president of the University of Oklahoma. She spent two years commuting from New York to eastern Oklahoma taking impressionistic photographs for this volume.

The evocative photographs of Daisy Decazes provide a fitting tribute to the natural beauty and the varied human resources of eastern Oklahoma. She has captured the fascinating interplay of land and people in a sensitive and imaginative way. Her photographs call forth the terrain and people of eastern Oklahoma in the same sense that stories of a favorite grandmother or uncle would bring out images of people and places long missed.

CARTER BLUE CLARK, Director of American Indian Studies
California State University, Long Beach

BETWEEN TWO WORLDS:
AN OKLAHOMA PERSPECTIVE

The tensions and conflicts in the Walker family over the last eighty years mirror the complex history of what has come to be known as Oklahoma.

My father's family, joined by several related families, moved to Indian Territory from the mountains of east Tennessee to buy "surplus" land in the Creek Nation. My grandfather, coming from a Union-supporting family, was firmly Republican. My father insisted that grandfather was "one-fifth of the Republican Party" in Fry Township, Tulsa County. It was clear that Joseph Dulaney Walker regarded the Democratic Party as the "party of succession," Jim Crow laws, and fiscal irresponsibility.

Coming to Broken Arrow, Indian Territory, as Cumberland Presbyterians, the Walkers joined the Methodist Episcopal Church. Joining the Methodist Episcopal Church, South was never an option. Grandfather regarded the M.E., South churchmen as "semi-pentecostal." This was, of course, a highly questionable claim. The real objection was his perception that M.E., South church members were southern sympathizers.

Educated as a lawyer at Cumberland University in Tennessee, J. D. Walker had been a schoolteacher, merchant, and lawyer "back home." He was, for a time, a partner in a general store in Broken Arrow and managed the local cotton gin. He gave up these pursuits to devote full time to farming and the importing of mules from Missouri for resale to the area's farmers.

J. D. Walker did not fit rural eastern Oklahoma stereo-

View from the Talimena drive, Kiamichi Mountain.

1

types in any form or fashion. Although he was adamantly opposed to Franklin D. Roosevelt and the New Deal, he was a man of great compassion and an uncanny sense of fairness. Even though he would not have understood the term, he was the community's "liberal." He was so in the sense that he had no use for the Jim Crow laws that were enacted shortly after statehood became a reality for Oklahoma. He gave legal counsel free of any cost or consideration to the area's whites, blacks, and Indians of modest means. Although not a spendthrift and often hard-pressed financially, he was as generous as possible to neighbors in need.

Grandfather, finally, all but abandoned his town home for the farm and life with the community's farming people. He made especially close friendships with a number of Creek families. My father and one uncle identified with their father in these matters. The other four children did not so identify and remained essentially "town bound" with their mother.

The mixed-blood Jackson-England side of the family did not welcome the Anglo and black newcomers to Indian Territory. This Cherokee, Scotch-Irish, and English family grouping opposed a willful federal government that forced the "allotment" property system on the five Indian republics. As more white settlers forced their way into Indian Territory with the aid and support of the federal government, the influence of the Jacksons and Englands waned, as was the case with many other Cherokee families.

The surplus land eagerly sought by the Walker family and their relatives was seen as land stolen from its rightful owners by my mother's clan. The Jackson and England families never recovered their influence after the coming of statehood for Oklahoma. This loss was never forgotten nor forgiven.

As Cherokee Baptists, fervent Democrats, southern sympathizers, and opponents of the allotment property system, there were areas of profound disagreement and tension between my mother's family and my father's kin. Religion, Oklahoma history, and political issues were seldom discussed at gatherings which included both sides of the family.

As the years proceeded, my paternal grandfather developed more and more sympathy for and understanding of his daughter-in-law's interpretation of Oklahoma history, as did my father and my favorite uncle. This was, however, not necessarily the case for the remaining members of the family. Joseph Dulaney Walker's views of F.D.R., the New Deal, religion, and the Jim Crow laws remained intact.

The hero of my mother's childhood was her grandfather, Benjamin C. England. A lay preacher, sheriff in the Cherokee Nation, farmer, and member of the Cherokee legislature, he was a beloved and respected member of his community. As a deputy United States marshal following statehood, he was involved in the pursuit of the Daltons and other legendary bandits of early Oklahoma.

One side of my mother's family, fearing the inability of the Cherokee Nation to withstand the onslaught of white settlers in the Southeast, moved with other Cherokee immigrants to what then was San Saba, Mexico. Texas at that time was a dependency of Old Mexico and was the domain claimed by the Comanche. These folk eventually made their way north and settled among the Cherokee people in Indian Territory.

The other side of my maternal clan resisted the forced removal of the Cherokee Nation from its homeland in the

Indian boy, Shawnee.

3

Southeast and, due to the relentless pressure of white settlers and the despicable behavior of white politicians, made their way to what would ultimately become eastern Oklahoma by means of the infamous Trail of Tears.

Mother's intellectual hero was Grant Foreman, the great historian of Indian removal. Due to a slow recovery from the Great Depression, money was in short supply on Walker's Hill in southern Tulsa County. Mother, even so, found the money to purchase every Foreman book. He alone, she was certain, knew the truth about Oklahoma history.

I well remember the day my mother read in the newspaper that Grant Foreman would be at a Tulsa bookstore to autograph copies of his books. She took my sister and me out of the grade school in Bixby to go meet the great man. As she drove us to Tulsa in a battered farm truck, I was certain I was on my way to meet the oracle of true knowledge. I was not disappointed in meeting my mother's hero.

THE STATE OF SEQUOYAH CONVENTION

At the dawn of the twentieth century, the five Indian republics that occupied most of Indian Territory attempted to fight the joining of Oklahoma and Indian territories to create the new State of Oklahoma. The State of Sequoyah Convention, made up of Indian Territory delegates, met in Muskogee in 1905. The proposed new state would be named in honor of the revered inventor of the Cherokee alphabet, Sequoyah. The name of the proposed new state was suggested by the Creek delegate, Alex Posey, the poet laureate of the Creek Nation.

Pleasant Porter, Principal Chief of the Creek Nation, led this last-ditch attempt of Indian tribal officials to gain admis-

Early morning mist on the Illinois River, north of Tahlequah.

Cypress trees in the fall, Beavers Bend State Park.

6

Indian paintbrush and butterfly, near Kinta.

sion of an Indian state comprised of the territory that made up Indian Territory. Republicans, anxious to avoid four new Democrat members of the United States Senate, opposed this move. The result of this and other opposition was the decision by Congress to admit a single state made up of the combined territories. The action of Congress ended the last desperate legal move to create an Indian state. The citizens of the former Indian republics were swamped by the new settlers. Non-Indians quickly came to dominate the new state politically.[1]

This text deals with this complex section of Oklahoma, eastern Oklahoma, the bulk of which would have become the State of Sequoyah had the Indian tribal leaders succeeded with their convention.

INDIAN REMOVAL

Prior to 1907, five self-governing Indian republics existed in what was called Indian Territory. The Cherokee, the Choctaw, the Chickasaw, the Creek or Muskogee, and Seminole nations shared Indian Territory with smaller tribes and fragments of tribes that had been removed to this new area, now eastern Oklahoma, to form an Indian section of the United States that would be safe from white European encroachment and domination. This was, at least, the theory supporting the removal of Indian people from their homelands to the new geographical and political entity known as Indian Territory.

The story of why Native American peoples were forced to abandon their homes and lands in order to move to Indian Territory is primarily one of white arrogance, greed, politics, and power. It is equally true that the dissolution of the

Indian republics is basically the story of white manipulative policy and power.[2] Large-scale Indian settlement in eastern Oklahoma was the result of such policy. Grant Foreman accurately suggests that this white policy consisted of formal negotiations, informal counsel, bribery, threats, and military force.[3]

As early as 1803, Thomas Jefferson spoke of a permanent Indian area or territory beyond the boundaries of white settlement.[4] President James Monroe and Secretary of War John C. Calhoun formed a plan for exiling the eastern Indian tribes to the trans-Mississippi West. The first "Trail of Tears," however, was not inflicted upon the Indian nations of the Southeast, but upon those tribes from the old Northwest, and, by 1825, virtually all the Native American peoples residing in the territory north of the Ohio River had been forced to relocate in the western wilderness.[5]

The Northwest Ordinance, ratified by Congress in 1789, stipulated that "The utmost good faith shall always be observed toward Indians; their land and property shall never be taken away from them without their consent." As the settlement of Indian Territory by non-Indians and the dissolution of the Indian republics made certain, the sentiments of documents such as the Northwest Ordinance proved to be mere pious platitudes easily cast aside in the face of white pressure for Indian land and political power over Indian people.

With the ascendance of Andrew Jackson in 1828, the federal government abandoned even the appearance of concern for Indian rights. Jackson and his successors threw aside even the pretense of conciliation with Native American people and pursued a relentless policy of removal and relocation. The practical result was the forced removal of the eastern tribes to the West.[6]

For 75 years, the history of Indian Territory was closely connected with the fortunes of five large tribes: Choctaw, Creek, Cherokee, Chickasaw, and Seminole. These peoples, known as the Five Civilized Tribes, lived, in the main, east of the Mississippi in 1830. They became acquainted with Europeans at an early date in the European colonization of North America. The consequence of this early contact and a receptiveness to many European cultural traditions produced new hybrid Indian cultures that borrowed selectively from the white man's ways while retaining dominant Indian social, economic, and cultural practices and attitudes.[7]

Because they were not citizens, the southern states did not have jurisdiction over the Five Civilized Nations. Each tribe had its own country, which had been guaranteed by the United States. The long and short of the matter was that American settlers wanted the rich lands belonging to the Indians and, by a variety of devices, reduced the political and military power of the Five Nations, took their land, and moved them westward.

The federal government completed the removal of most of the southern Indians to eastern Oklahoma during the decade of the 1830s. Their removal is called, aptly, the Trail of Tears. The migrating Indians experienced incredible hardships and suffering. This author's great-great-grandfather survived the ordeal. Many Indian people were on the trail in midwinter. They were exposed to freezing temperatures with inadequate food or shelter. Few wagons were provided, and those were reserved for the very young, the old and feeble, the sick, and the blind. Cholera, smallpox, and measles epidemics took many, many lives. Each of the Five Nations was thought to have lost at least one-fourth of its population as a consequence of the forced march.[8]

The Trail of Tears is the "exodus event" around which history revolves for the descendents of those who survived the trip west. A visit to virtually any exhibition of the work of Indian painters with ancestral ties to the five tribes will contain a significant number of interpretations of the unhappiness that marked the march westward.

The feeling of the Creeks about this experience was summed up in a letter written to their "conductor" (the Army officer responsible for "conducting" the Creek people on their journey to what would become eastern Oklahoma):

> You have heard the cries of our men, women, and children.... We wanted to gather our crops, and we want to go in peace and friendship. Did we? No! We were drove off like wolves ... lost our crops ... and our people's feet were bleeding with long marches.[9]

Perhaps more than 40 percent of the Creek population was lost during and immediately after the experience of removal. The once powerful Creek Nation would never fully recover from this wretched experience.[10]

The Creeks sought to deal with the awful fact of removal in an orderly manner. They gathered their livestock and other property and prepared to move to their new homes. Before they had finished their preparations for the long journey, white settlers invaded their Alabama lands. The Creeks, rightly, defended their homes and drove off the invading settlers. The greedy intruders sought protection from the angry Indians. The federal government, ever anxious to protect the white settlers, sent troops to the Creek Nation. The

White-tailed deer, Osage County.

Great blue heron, Mountain Fork River.

soldiers arrested many Creek defenders, placed them in shackles and chains, and drove them with bayonets to Indian Territory.[11]

The Chickasaw and Choctaw removals were the most orderly. Members of these tribes, however, lost livestock and other property along the way. Disease epidemics struck these people during their journeys, causing much suffering and many deaths.[12]

The Cherokee, Creek, and Seminole removals were the most conflict-ridden. Many members of these nations were determined not to bow to white power and theft.[13] Some Cherokees, for example, escaped into the gorges and thick forests of the Great Smoky Mountains where they became the nucleus of the eastern Cherokee, but most were either killed or rounded up and set off on their long, bitter march.[14]

Many Seminoles also defied the federal army by escaping into the Georgia/Florida swamps and, thus, escaped deportation to Indian Territory.

For a number of years, beginning as early as the 1790s, a voluntary exile had been undertaken by several factions of the eastern tribes. To escape white cultural and political domination, small bands of Indians had been moving west of the Mississippi River into what then was Spanish territory. In addition to factions of the Cherokee and Chickasaw, large numbers of Shawnees, Delawares, and Kickapoos moved west and settled on land provided by Spain.[15]

Most southern Indians were, however, determined to retain their ancestral lands and sought to protect their right to remain in the East. One strategy was coexistence. They studiously supported American foreign policy. These efforts in-

volved, ironically, the raising of a regiment of fighting men which joined Maj. Gen. Andrew Jackson's army to guard the southwestern frontier against British invasion.[16]

In order to accommodate themselves to European ways, many Creek, Cherokee, Choctaw, and Chickasaw leaders initially urged their people to adopt white customs in dress and industry. The Indians, as a consequence, established successful farms, plantations, and businesses in their nations. Many Indian farmers and plantation owners became prosperous slave owners. They changed their political systems from traditional tribal governments to governments based on written constitutions with elective officials, courts, and other elements of enlightened Anglo-American polity.[17]

The Creeks, Cherokees, Choctaws, and Chickasaws established schools, often with the assistance of missionary organizations, and sent many young people to collegiate institutions in the Northeast to continue their educations. Each Indian nation quickly developed a corps of elitist leaders, more often than not, better educated than their white counterparts in the Southeast. These rapid advances gained them ugly envy and antagonism from their southeastern Anglo-American neighbors. Instead of acceptance, the "civilized" Indians were increasingly perceived as a threat.[18]

Instead of acceptance, the acculturated Indians were daily subjected to brutalities and atrocities by white neighbors, harassed by white-controlled state governments, cajoled and bribed by federal agents to agree to removal, and denied even the basic protection of the federal government.[19]

The slaves of the southern Indians were also subjected to the agony of removal. They did much of the hardest work on the trail, loading freight wagons and tending livestock.

Black workers were forced to clear roads for the overland march. These individuals suffered the rigors of the journey with their masters and arrived along with the Indian pioneers of Indian Territory.[20]

The strategy of southern whites was, simply, to drive the Indians out of their states and to utilize the federal political and military structure to accomplish this goal. Despite federal treaties with the nations that pledged governmental protection of Indian rights and property, the southern whites succeeded in removing almost all sign of Indians from their states.[21] President Jackson sealed the fate of the eastern Indians by utterly refusing to acknowledge the federal government's responsibility to protect Indians from state and informal white action. Jackson's refusal to uphold the United States Supreme Court's decision in 1832, in the case of *Worcester* v. *Georgia,* destroyed the southern Indians' last hope of federal protection of their legal and moral rights.

The once powerful Osage Nation was reduced to a much smaller area in Indian Territory. The Osages, Quapaws, Senecas, Shawnees, Peorias, Modocs, Ottawas, Wyandottes, Tonkawas, Poncas, Ottos, Missouris, Pottawatomies, Kickapoos, Pawnees, Iowas, Sac and Fox, and the Kaws were removed to eastern Oklahoma and became parts of the new "Indian Country."

THE INDIAN REPUBLICS AND INDIAN TERRITORY

Four of the Five Civilized Tribes adopted written constitutions following many Anglo-American legal practices. Emerging from these cross-cultural experiments were inde-

Canoeing in the fall, Beavers Bend State Park.

14

Dogwood and redbuds, Honor Heights Park, Muskogee.

Horseback riders, Illinois River, Cookson Hills.

pendent Indian republics that fostered a native farming class and an educated business and professional class. The republics established public school systems teaching in both English and Native American languages, as well as public mental health facilities, newspapers, schoolbooks, political parties, organizations, and religious groupings. They borrowed from the white world and retained much of their valued Indian culture.[22]

Rennard Strickland provides a very helpful summary of the sociocultural heritage that was retained by the populations of the Five Nations in the following statement.

> The ownership of land in common and the shared use of tribal resources were continued. Many of the most important elements of tribal culture, such as respect for the land, shared obligation for the welfare of fellow tribesmen, and the regard for the rights of women, were preserved. Other traditions merged in a society that provided a maximum of freedom to pursue either traditional Indian or white cultural variations.[23]

The attack on the common ownership of land by land-hungry non-Indians, with the support of the federal government, would prove the means by which the five Indian republics were dissolved as geographical dependent states.

The new settlers making up the five Indian republics emerged from the experience of exploitation and removal with the most invincible determination to maintain their tribal autonomy in the West against encroachments of territorial or state governments and to continue common tribal property holdings against the European system of land ownership.[24] The behavior of the southern states was ever fresh

Reflection in a pond, near Okmulgee.

18

in the minds of the citizens of Indian Territory. In 1829, Mississippi extended state laws to cover Choctaw and Chickasaw lands and made Indians citizens of the state. Indian citizens were forbidden, under penalty of fine and imprisonment, to hold any tribal office. Georgia did the same: forbidding tribal legislatures from meeting save to ratify land cessions. This invited white citizens to rob and plunder their Indian neighbors at will by making it illegal for an Indian to bring suit or testify against a white man.[25] A resolution developed among the Indian people of Indian Territory never to allow these humiliating experiences to repeat themselves.

Approximately the size of South Carolina and almost the size of Indiana, the Indian republics contained excellent agricultural land, valuable timber resources, extensive coal fields, and great reservoirs of oil and gas. Each tribe formed an intensely nationalistic republic with distinctive customs and socio-political institutions. The Creeks and Seminoles proved to be the most conservative, but the other three tribes were eagerly receptive to other customs and practices which they considered superior to their own.[26]

Despite some initial hostility, especially among the Creeks, the tribes converted to Christianity at a rapid pace following removal. Naturally a people with devout mystical feelings, a deep sense of moral obligation, and family and group solidarity, the citizens of the Indian republics found Christian teachings suited their own thought patterns. The Indian settlements had their Presbyterian, Methodist, or Baptist churches. A few missionaries continued to work in Indian Territory, but most of their clergy were Indian, a number with college educations.[27]

Each republic operated its school system without federal participation or interference. In addition to elementary schools, no better or worse than those in the neighboring states of the Union, each tribe maintained several boarding schools with well-qualified faculty, and at least one tribe paid the expenses of selected young people to study at the great universities of the country. As a result of these educational endeavors, there was a larger proportion of educated people among the Cherokees, Choctaws, and Chickasaws than among the white people of the neighboring states. Even so, considerable illiteracy remained so far as knowledge of English was concerned.[28]

With the possible exception of the Seminoles, about whom little is known in this connection, practically all Indian citizens in the five republics were accustomed to reading books and newspapers in their own language. The United States maintained a protectorate over these Indian republics. The rights of each were based on an elaborate system of land treaties. Although it long had been a recognized principle of law that Congress could abrogate a treaty by statute, the federal officials up to 1890 showed some decent hesitation about breaking their legal pledges to the Five Civilized Tribes. The Indian leaders, having consumed the bitter cup of federal and state legal dominance, quoted the treaties with such skill and fluency that they invariably outdebated their white opponents.[29]

The political leadership of the Five Nations, who were often better educated than the governors and legislators of the neighboring states of Texas and Arkansas, promoted better education among their peoples for many reasons, including that of attempting to fend off the ever-encroaching world of white America.[30] The missionaries, to their credit,

Indian boy, intertribal powwow, Shawnee.

Cows in the early morning, north of Tahlequah.

On the Dilingham Ranch, Okmulgee County.

Rounding up cattle, Dilingham Ranch, Okmulgee County.

24

Winter morning on the Dilingham Ranch, Okmulgee County.

25

Old man and house, near Ada.

26

Dinner on the grounds, Wheelock Church, near Millerton.

Noon shade, near Jay.

28

often encouraged Indian leaders in their nationalistic development, advising them to stand up for their own interests against those of whites.[31]

One large group of Indian people outside the governing systems of the Five Nations and occupying a large section of eastern Oklahoma following the Civil War was the Osages. They were steadfast in their resistance to white influence. They rejected "civilized" customs with fierce determination. In the nineteenth century they refused to lay down their Osage garb or to lose the habits of the hunter and the warrior. Faced with a changing world, even the nineteenth-century Osage were forced to change.[32]

Like the southern state governments, the Indian governments recognized and supported the ownership of black slaves. On farms, plantations, and ranches of Indian Territory, Indian people lived much like other people of the South. Commerce was carried on largely with the markets in southern cities: Memphis, Shreveport, and New Orleans. At the beginning of the Civil War, most of the Indian agents and officers of the United States operating in Indian Territory were from the South, and many transferred their loyalty to the government of the Confederate States of America without great emotional difficulty.[33]

Many Indian leaders wanted their nations to remain neutral concerning this new "white man's war." The troops of the Confederate States of America easily took control of Indian Territory as the troops of the United States retreated in the face of greater, unbeatable numbers. Early in May, 1861, Indian Territory was abandoned by the federal army, and it was immediately organized as a part of a Confederate States Military District. By the fall of 1861, all of the Indian nations had made treaties with the rebel government.

A significant number of Indians remained loyal to the Union. Civil wars were fought within several of the nations, most notably among the Creeks and Seminoles, and the consequences were bloody and severe. Among the Cherokees who opposed the Confederate cause were the Keetoowah, members of a traditionalist secret society which favored the abolition of slavery. The Choctaws and Chickasaws were the most united in their support of the Confederate States of America.

Brig. Gen. Stand Watie, a Cherokee Confederate leader and the only Indian Civil War general, was the implacable enemy of Union Indians. Watie was the last Confederate general to surrender and accept the Union victory. Despite the official involvement on the side of the South in the conflict and Watie's leadership, more Cherokees served in the Union army than in the Confederate army. The same was true for the Creek Nation.

The Indian Territory as originally conceived did not long remain intact. The federal government in 1855 leased the southwestern portion of Indian Territory from the Choctaws and Chickasaws, designated it the Leased District and colonized several tribes from Texas on the land.[34]

Non-Indian settlers soon began making their familiar demands that Indian lands be opened to them. By 1850 these would-be settlers were thrusting against Indian Territory. Always far more sensitive to majority voter pressure than solemn treaty pledges of permanent tenure and occupancy of Indian Territory, federal officials wasted little time in succumbing to the demands of the non-Indian settlers aiming to settle in Indian Territory. In 1850 several bills were introduced in Congress providing for the opening of Indian Territory land to settlement and for the creation of several new civil territories. Settler pressure triumphed to a significant degree when in 1854 Congress enacted the Kansas-Nebraska Act which opened the northern one-half of Indian Territory and created the new civil territories of Kansas and Nebraska. Most of the Indian lands in this portion of Kansas and Nebraska were liquidated.[35]

During the war a political movement for relocation of Indian peoples developed, led by Samuel C. Pomeroy and James H. Lane, United States senators from Kansas. These white political leaders sought to move the Osage, Pottawatomie, Kickapoo, Sac and Fox, Ottawa, Kansas, Iowa, and Shawnee tribes to Indian Territory. Pomeroy, Lane, and other white political operatives sought to open land in Indian Territory for the relocation of the tribal groups just named. Land was taken from the Five Nations and given to the new Indian settlers on the theory that they had, as a consequence, lost their treaty rights.[36]

The Civil War left Indian Territory a region of desolation. Although few broadly decisive battles were fought within its area, the entire population had been involved, and the destruction of homes, public structures, crops and fences, livestock, tools and implements had been almost complete. Public education declined significantly throughout the Five Nations. Schools had been used as barracks and hospitals, and in such cases the retreating army almost invariably burned them. Tribal finances were equally low during the Reconstruction period, and the heavy cost of rebuilding schools made the process of doing so very slow.[37]

Like the nation as a whole, the Indian nations displayed a tendency toward low political standards after the Civil War, and bribes given by federal officials to Indian political leaders were not unknown.[38]

There is no doubt that the Five Nations of Indian Territory paid more dearly than any other peoples or governments for their involvement on the losing side of the Civil War. This involvement became a convenient excuse for legalizing greater white encroachment and power in Indian Territory.

The winter of 1866 saw the Five Nations make new treaties with the United States that reduced their sovereignty and limited their freedom of self-government. The plan for each nation to give up its lands in western Indian Territory, which had been begun by the federal government before the civil conflict, was now made a part of the new treaties. Only the eastern one-half of Indian Territory remained the country of the Five Civilized Tribes.[39]

Each of the treaties of 1866 contained similar provisions. Slavery was abolished, and the freedmen were to be given their rights of citizenship in the Indian republics; right-of-ways for the construction of railroads were granted; an intertribal council made up of representatives of every tribe and nation was to be organized. The agency was to organize one government within the boundaries of Indian Territory. This last demand was, of course, the first bold step toward a goal that finally resulted in the organization of the State of Oklahoma 40 years later.[40]

Beginning with 1869, bills were introduced in Congress providing for the organization of Indian Territory as a federal territory with the name of "Oklahoma," from two Choctaw words, *Okla,* meaning "red," and *homma* (or *humma*) meaning "people." The literal meaning "Territory of Okla-

Horseshoeing at the Fort Gibson stockade.

homa" was "Territory of Red People." For many years these bills failed to pass. Finally in 1890, a bill known as the "Organic Act" was passed by Congress. This piece of federal legislation provided that the western part of Indian Territory should be organized as "Oklahoma Territory."[41] The passage of the Organic Act was an ominous step toward ending Indian sovereignty in the "promised land in the West."

The Civil War ended the "golden age" of Indian economic, social, political, and education development in Indian Territory. From that point it was a series of rearguard battles to fight off new thrusts by non-Indians into Indian Territory.

The most basic Indian conventions were now under attack, especially the common ownership of the land within each of the five republics. In 1874 the leaders of the Osage Nation issued a "protest against the establishment by Congress of a Territorial Government of the United States, over the Indian Nations." One of the consequences of the new treaties and territorial status was the loss of 23,000 acres of Indian lands to the railroads.[42]

Indians in the five republics developed a novel economic middle-ground position in terms of land development and use. Indian farmers and ranchers were encouraged to develop tracts of land on an individualistic, capitalistic basis. These individuals determined the use of the profits of their labor. The farmers and ranchers could, however, own only the improvements constructed on the property. If an individual or family abandoned property, it reverted to the communal landholdings of the republic.

The year 1889 was when white farmers came with their families in great numbers to what had been Indian land. Until that fateful year, although subject to many federal

The largest United States flag, McAlester.

The cannon, Fort Washita.

Memorial Day, Fort Gibson National Cemetery.

regulations, Indians owned all the lands that were to become Oklahoma. Whites within this area were there with Indian permission or were government or military officials. Illegal intruders were subject to expulsion under existing treaties. The land rush of '89 brought non-Indians in large numbers to previously Indian controlled territory.[43]

Rennard Strickland sums up the political movements aimed at reducing and, finally, eliminating Indian sovereignty in Oklahoma in the following statement:

> By 1871 the treaty era had finally ended, and even the pretense of a negotiated equality had been replaced by terrorizing potential of executive order and congressional governance.[44]

As Indian leaders coped with the consequences of the treaties of 1866 and the Railroad Act of July 26, 1866, they understood fully the determination of the railroad companies to secure land grants at the expense of the Five Nations. They also faced the unhappy fact that the coming of the railroads to Indian Territory meant new non-Indian settlers in their midst. It was, of course, in the economic interests of the railroads to open Indian lands to non-Indian settlers, to increase the population of Indian Territory, and, thereby, to increase potential rail traffic and profits.

Towns grew along the railroad tracks, trade increased, and citizens from the states began to settle in the Five Nations. Some of the "temporary" residents were employed by the railroads and others leased property from the Indian owners in the towns and set up business concerns. Non-Indian farmers came into Indian Territory and opened farms and ranches by lease contracts with individual Indian citizens. These folk were to be subject to the laws of the nations and were to pay fees each year for permits to remain in the Indian republics. With the passing of the years and the increase of white population, many new settlers failed to pay the required permit fees to the Indian governments.[45]

A large number of the new immigrants in Indian Territory were legal residents, who conformed in good faith to the laws of the Indian governments and whose productive labor and skills were desired by the Indians. All the nations had experienced intermarriage. Intermarried whites were more often than not admitted to citizenship. There had been considerable mixture of white blood in all the tribes before removal, but, for a time after the move west, white influence and intermarriage almost disappeared. The coming of the railroads to the Five Nations and the greater population in the western states produced renewed immigration by non-Indians into Indian Territory and intermarriage. Each nation dealt with the problem of intermarried whites differently.[46]

A far more serious problem for the Indian republics was the non-citizen, non-intermarried, non-Indian immigration that, as Angie Debo correctly stated, "began as a trickle into Indian Territory soon after the Civil War and became a deluge that engulfed the Indian settlements by the close of the century."[47] Many blacks entered the nations as laborers in the mines or as tenants on Indian farms. Large numbers of immigrants were simply intruders, who entered and remained in Indian Territory as lawless intruders. It is difficult to overestimate the disruption to the Indian republics caused by the unwelcome and unprincipled white rabble that took up unlawful residence in the Five Nations.

It was not long before the Indian citizens were outnum-

Reflection in the window, Boley.

bered in Indian Territory. By 1890, the Creeks, Choctaws, Cherokees, Chickasaws, and Seminoles were a minority in their own republics. This flood of non-Indian immigrants produced a population of great diversity of nationality, education, occupation, and creed, with few interests in common.[48] Of the people living in Indian Territory in 1890, 178,097 were non-Indian and 50,055 were Indian.[49]

Following Indian custom and preference, all the land in the Five Nations was held under communal tenure. Citizens could, as has been suggested, cultivate as much land as they wanted, and the laws of the nations protected their rights of occupancy and the possession of improvements; but as soon as individuals ceased to use the land, the title reverted to the nation. Although this deep-seated tradition of communal tenure was contrary to the individualistic white man, the Indian people of the Five Nations operated their affairs with this convention in a manner that produced contentment and economic prosperity.[50]

Non-Indians lived in the Indian republics without the ability to secure title to land they cultivated and paid taxes to support a government in which they had no voice and a school system that did not serve them. The fact that their living arrangements rested upon the most solemn commitments made by the federal government and that they had voluntarily subjected themselves to these conditions was most often ignored. The practical result of the dissatisfaction of the white "guests" in Indian Territory was a constant clamor for the abolition of the Indian governments and the establishment of a governmental system representative of the whole population. Another demand of the white settlers, accepted by the federal government and which caused radical

disruption to the socioeconomic practices of the Indian republics, was for the transformation of the communal landholding system into that of individual tenure that would allow non-Indian ownership.[51]

Congress did away with communal landholding, a system that produced prosperity when operated by Indian people who deeply respected the convention, because of white political pressure and opposition based on ideological belief in the sanctity of private ownership. Investigation of the actual socioeconomic circumstances in the Five Nations or any serious exploration of the Indian mind-set toward the use of land was unnecessary in face of the convincing force of economic ideology in this matter.[52]

In 1893, Congress provided for the appointment of a commission of three members to make new agreements with the Indian republics that were to provide: 1) for the removal of Indian title to lands; 2) for the abandonment of the Indian governments; 3) for adjustment of Indian affairs to prepare Indian Territory for admission into the Union; and 4) for the allotment of land in severalty, which meant that a certain amount of land was to be allowed each member of the Five Civilized Tribes.[53] The Dawes Commission gave oversight to the death of one of the most deeply valued Indian traditions, that of communal landholding, and to the transfer of great amounts of land from Indian ownership to non-Indian ownership.

The new system of private landownership has not promoted the prosperity for Indian people in eastern Oklahoma that its theoretical advocates claimed would inevitably be the case. The 20 million acres of land that made up the Five Nations that was marked by general prosperity on the part of

Going to the parade, Miami.

First American family, Miami.

its Indian citizens are now marked by significant contrasts of prosperity and poverty.

One armed rebellion, that of the Crazy Snake Creeks led by Chitto Harjo, defied the federal courts and army in its efforts to destroy the system of tribally owned lands by alloting land units of 160-acre allotments, including blacks, women, and children, to individual Creek citizens. Harjo spoke these understandable words in his own defense: "At that time we had these troubles, it was to take my country away from me. I had no other troubles, I could live in peace with all else, but they wanted my country and I was in trouble defending it."[54]

The Curtis Act of 1898 dealt a further blow to the Indian republics by abolishing the tribal court system. All laws passed by the tribal legislatures, henceforth, had to be approved by the President of the United States. The tribal governments were to close on March 4, 1906. In 1906, Congress approved allowing the Indian governments to operate until March 4, 1907. The Five Tribes Act of 1906 allowed the governments of the Five Nations to continue to exist without coercive powers, with the principal chief or governor and tribal legislatures being appointed by the federal government.

The Indian-created and operated school systems were also doomed by the new political order. The Choctaw Council, for instance, protested the interference of the Secretary of the Interior in the Choctaw educational system. By assuming control of the mineral royalties, which had been controlled by the Choctaw national government, the federal government deprived the Choctaw Nation of the resources to support any school system. The Department of the Interior took over full control of the Choctaw schools, finally allowing for a Choctaw advisor to be appointed to assist the supervisor of schools. The boarding schools, once the pride of the Choctaw nation, became vocational schools for the training of fullbloods.[55]

Statehood was a bitter pill for many, if not most, citizens of the former Indian republics. The author's mother and her family found it difficult to celebrate the advent of statehood for Oklahoma. Rather than a point in history to celebrate as a mark of achievement, it was a very sad time when geographical nationhood was lost for the Five Nations.

One apparently true story, related by historian Edward Everett Dale, holds that a Cherokee woman married to a white man refused to attend the statehood ceremonies with her husband. He returned and said to her: "Well, Mary, we no longer live in the Cherokee Nation. All of us are now citizens of the State of Oklahoma." Tears came to her eyes 30 years later as she recalled that day. "It broke my heart. I went to bed and cried all night long. It seemed more than I could bear that the Cherokee Nation, my country and my people's country, was no more."[56]

An elderly Creek man in a nursing home in Broken Arrow, Oklahoma, in 1969, volunteered abruptly, in the middle of a conversation with this writer that, "1907 was the saddest year for my family." Rennard Strickland is correct when he suggests that, "few whites ever understood the depth of Indian agony at the passing of nationhood."[57]

"We spoiled the best territory in the world to make a state," Will Rogers ironically joked. A state like Oklahoma was inevitable, Rogers said, because, "Indians were so cruel they were all killed by civilized white men for encroaching

Watching the parade, Stilwell.

Queen of the Strawberry Festival, Stilwell.

On the telephone, Boley.

Going to the rodeo, Boley.

45

On the campaign trail with Ross Swimmer, Principal Chief of the Western Cherokee Nation.

Observers at Cherokee political rally, Sequoyah County.

on white domain."[58]

This lack of enthusiasm for statehood continues into the present. Ninety-seven-year-old Joanna Parris, one of the few living great-grandchildren of the venerable Cherokee leader and Principal Chief John Ross, made clear how many, if not most, Cherokees felt about the advent of statehood in a January 13, 1985, *Muskogee Phoenix* interview:

> "We wasn't glad because the Dawes Commission come, you know," she said. "I was standing out in the yard when they run by and said statehood had been declared. We wasn't glad."[59]

THE NEW STATE

Probably no other state in the Union was settled so rapidly by so many people from different parts of the United States as was the new State of Oklahoma. Southeast Oklahoma, known as "Little Dixie," was settled by people from the South: Tennessee, Alabama, Georgia, and Arkansas in the main. They brought their social traditions, populist Democrat politics, and culture with them to Oklahoma.

The northern part of the old Indian Territory saw an influx of settlers from the Midwest and Northeast. Bartlesville and Tulsa became home to significant numbers of people from the northeastern industrial states. These new citizens were often brought to Oklahoma by the oil concerns that employed them to develop Oklahoma's newly discovered oil and gas resources. In addition to settlers from both North and South, newcomers of northern European stock came to farm the western Oklahoma "shortgrass country."

Regional differences within the state were more obvious before the 1950s. To a child growing to adulthood on the

Passing time, Nowata.

49

plains and in the rolling hills of the western half of the state, the forty-sixth state was a land of wheat and cotton fields and cattle. Although farmers were numerically dominant, the more romantic cowboy was the preeminent symbol in western Oklahoma and the Panhandle counties. A child growing up in the hills and valleys of eastern Oklahoma, however, more likely grew up in a family and social context whose diet, manners, and life-style reflected the ways of the South.

The southern settlers won the day politically and socially in the new state. Jim Crow laws were soon the law of the land in Oklahoma, and rigid segregation was the norm. Indians, unlike in Mississippi, were exempt from the convention of segregation. Latins and Orientals were also allowed to attend white schools.

Following the Civil War, the Indian nations had to accept their former slaves and give them land. The practice of segregation preceded the new white settlers from the South. The southern states segregated their former slaves following the War Between the States, and the Five Nations copied this unhappy practice. Blacks were forced to live in settlements apart from the Indian towns. All-black communities such as Boley, Foreman, Red Bird, and Rentiesville developed as a consequence of the segregating laws passed by the Indian legislatures. The tribal governments also adopted laws segregating black children in schools.[60]

Nearly 1,000 blacks, most of them from the South, made the Run of 1889. Many blacks sought and obtained the desired homesteads, and most settled east of Guthrie. Langston was established by these settlers as an all-black community.[61]

Not surprisingly, a new secret organization, called the Ku Klux Klan, gained popularity in Oklahoma. It was first organized in about 1920 and included both white and Indian members. In addition to making sure that Oklahoma's blacks knew and kept "their place," the KKK promoted itself as an agent of law and order in the often lawless Oklahoma oil fields and boom towns. Gov. John C. Walton, much to his credit, warned county officials that such persons were as lawless as the lawbreakers they sought to punish. Trouble from lawlessness and whippings by men in disguise, nonetheless, continued.[62]

Arousing great opposition, Governor Walton placed several counties under martial law, including Tulsa County. A massacre of black citizens in the form of a race riot had taken place in Tulsa in 1921, and sporadic violence continued into Walton's brief term. Soon the whole state was placed under martial law, though it was enforced in only a few areas.

Although impeached by the Oklahoma legislature, Walton had made his point, and the Ku Klux Klan has yet to be revived in any significant manner in Oklahoma. Governor Walton was later returned to public office by his fellow citizens by being elected as a member of the State Corporation Commission.

The State of Sequoyah movement failed, but the Sequoyah constitution was to become the model for the Oklahoma constitution: some provisions were adopted word for word. Largely a populist document with progressive sub-themes, the Oklahoma constitution reflected both Southern and Midwestern Agrarian Populism. William H. "Alfalfa" Bill Murray, the Sage of Tishomingo, was the colorful and influential theoretician of both the Sequoyah and Oklahoma constitu-

Cub Scouts, Stilwell.

50

Coffee break, Stigler.

Stocking up, Bartlesville.

tions. He was to serve as speaker of the state's House of Representatives, as a member of its congressional delegation, and as Oklahoma's ninth governor.[63]

In the amazing political career of Alfalfa Bill Murray, one sees the clear triumph of Southern Agrarian Populism as the dominant political and social force during the first 30 years of the new State of Oklahoma. "I hold," Governor Murray would state time and time again in his vigorous, but ill-fated, quest for the 1932 Democratic Party presidential nomination, "that civilization begins and ends with the plow; that no government can stand without freedom for the farmer, from physical and financial slavery. . . . Virgin wealth comes only from agriculture, the mines, and other natural resources."[64] Murray's presidential campaign song, "The Land Calls for a Man From Dixie," illustrates the victory of the new state's predominant Southern Populist identity over the competing southwestern influence.[65]

Regional differences have been blurred in Oklahoma. The influence and spread of radio and television, linking the population of the state more closely into one unit by means of regular statewide news broadcasts, reduced regional differences. Better roads and highways also helped prompt the evolution of a greater statewide consciousness and identity, as formerly remote areas were opened to outside influences.

A PROFOUND CHANGE OF IDENTITY

With the passing of federal legislation in 1955 requiring the desegregation of public education in all the states of the Union came the most far-reaching contemporary social change in eastern Oklahoma. Orval Faubus of Arkansas, Ross Barnett of Mississippi, and George Wallace of Alabama led the southern efforts to defy federal mandate to desegregate the segregated public schools in the South and Southwest.

Oklahoma was fortunate to have a thoughtful governor from "Little Dixie" in office at this crucial time. Instead of opting for the role of the gubernatorial racial demagogue, Gov. Raymond Gary opted for constructive, peaceful desegregation.

It is difficult not to appreciate the importance of the fact that Governor Gary was an active Southern Baptist layman from Oklahoma's most socially conservative section. The Southern Baptist Convention was possibly in its most socially constructive period during Raymond Gary's tenure as the state's chief executive. The example of an active Southern Baptist layman acting in a peaceful, thoughtful manner in the midst of extreme social change was not lost on his co-religionists. The Southern Baptists were and are, by far, the largest religious grouping in Oklahoma.

Another positive factor in this potentially volatile situation was the fact that the Women's Society of Christian Service of the Methodist Church, now the United Methodist Church, engaged itself in a nationwide study of the biblical basis of segregation and concluded that such practices were both socially and theologically wrong. The Women's Society of Christian Service of the Methodist Church in Oklahoma actively participated in this study that was undertaken in virtually all of the state's cities, towns, and hamlets. The Methodist community of faith was and is Oklahoma's second largest religious grouping.

Governor Gary issued an executive order to desegregate the schools in Oklahoma. Working with a state legislature

Dominoes at the Smoke House, Pawhuska.

Citizens of the Cherokee Nation, Sequoyah County.

whose loyalty to the governor was at an all-time high, Gary quietly laid the groundwork for desegregation by contacting local school boards to gain their support and by calling on both the small town and metropolitan press to "downplay" any disturbances that might occur during the transition from segregation in the schools to the new desegregated situation.[66] While almost all southern states experienced rioting, mob protests, boycotts, bombings, and temporary school closings, Oklahoma peacefully desegregated its schools.

The first school in Oklahoma to desegregate was in eastern Oklahoma, Poteau, and the second was also in the old State of Sequoyah, Madill. Madill is the home of the Raymond Gary family.

Clergy, judicial officers, school administrators and boards, business and civic leaders worked long and hard through the gubernatorial administrations of J. Howard Edmondson and Henry Bellmon to avoid the civil discord that marked the desegregation of the public schools, public accommodations, employment patterns, etc., in so many sections of the previously rigidly segregated South. It is impossible to name all the heros of these amazingly successful efforts to effect significant social change in a peaceful and constructive manner. These individuals, needless to say, often experienced difficulty and hostility as they carried out their important civic duties. All Oklahomans remain in their debt for thoughtful persistence in the midst of a potentially volatile situation.

The second major civil rights test for Oklahoma was to come with the passage of the 1964 Civil Rights Act. Prior to this date many public accommodations and tax-supported institutions, with the exception of schools, colleges, and universities, remained segregated. There was never a doubt in the mind of the state's first Republican governor, Henry Bellmon, that the state government would do everything in its power to prompt compliance wih the various provisions of the 1964 Civil Rights Act.[67]

On the day following the signing of the Civil Rights Act, Governor Bellmon conducted a lengthy staff meeting concerning compliance with the public accommodations section of the new federal legislation. No consensus emerged from the meeting concerning compliance strategy. Following a late afternoon press conference at which the question of compliance did not arise, Bellmon told his legal counsel, H. Dale Cook, that he would fly to Idabel that evening and back to Hugo the next morning. These two communities are located deep in the "Little Dixie" section of the state.

Clara Luper, an Oklahoma City civil rights leader, was threatening to take carloads of young civil rights activists to southeastern Oklahoma to test compliance wih the public accommodations provisions of the Civil Rights Act. There were fears that such action would stiffen resistance to the social changes required by the new legislation. There were also fears that police activity or use of the National Guard might be needed to enforce compliance and keep the peace.

Idabel area restaurant, hotel, and motel owners and operators were invited by Virgil Jumper, banker and member of the Oklahoma State Highway Commission, to meet with Governor Bellmon. Albert Cherry, a member of the Oklahoma Turnpike Authority, invited like persons to participate in a similar meeting in Hugo. In these meetings, without press coverage and fanfare, Bellmon secured pledges of cooperation and compliance.

Clara Luper and Bill Rose, Director of Oklahoma Human

58

The law, Boley.

At the celebration, Nowata.

The Sorghum Festival, Wewoka.

60

Strawberry auction at the festival, Stilwell.

Starting the day, Boley.

62

Rights Commission, drove to southeastern Oklahoma to test compliance and returned to Oklahoma City with positive reports that were given at the press conference. Restaurant, hotel, and motel owners over the state, with few exceptions, followed the good example set by their counterparts in Hugo and Idabel.

The strategy devised by the inventive Henry Bellmon defused possible awkward responses to the public accommodations portions of the 1964 Civil Rights Act and provided the state with examples of thoughtful compliance. Oklahoma was fortunate to have discerning and constructive chief examples in both 1954 and 1964. Their exemplary behavior helped the state pass through a period of significant social change without large-scale public disruptions or defiance of federal court decisions and congressional action.

"Bull" Connor, Police Commissioner of Birmingham, Alabama, also contributed to peaceful desegregation in Oklahoma. The crudity of Connor's actions and the nationwide negative reaction to the nature of his professional behavior and his personal attitudes prompted many Oklahomans to put new distance between themselves and the southern side of their identity.

The crudeness of Connor, Wallace, Barnett, Faubus, etc., and the general portrayal by the national media of the American South as being socially and economically backward caused a profound change of identity in Oklahoma and on the part of Oklahomans. Anxious to attract new industry and concerned to appear progressive and modern, Oklahoma's leaders opted to tilt dramatically in favor in the "western" side of the state's dual image.

This tilt in favor of a western/southwestern identity is nowhere more evident than in the public relations material of the Oklahoma City Chamber of Commerce. This material highlights Oklahoma City as the home of the National Cowboy Hall of Fame, as the location at the center of a large concentration of American Indians, and as a center of rodeo activity, the raising and selling of horses, and horse shows. This image is equally evident in the tourist publications of the State of Oklahoma and in the public relations materials of the great majority of the state's chambers of commerce and civic organizations.

One of the fundamental distinctions of Oklahoma is the clear tendency to exhibit affection in the form of humor and teasing. Contrary to the movie and television portrayal of Native Americans, Indian people in Oklahoma are given to humorous discourse and good-natured teasing. Will Rogers and Oklahoma City University's highly successful basketball coach/humorist, Abe Lemons, are proof positive of this tendency.

The following story related by Gid Graham, proud part-Cherokee, wildlife conservationist, and member of the Oklahoma State Senate, provides an excellent example of Oklahoma's distinctive sense of humor.

> Unable to live with my children, whose habits were different than mine, I finally decided to marry again. Mrs. Misamore was 50 years old and had been associated with my wife and children for several years; my children held her in the highest esteem. Our association developed into love, and I decided it would be the wise thing to marry.
>
> After our decision to get married, I asked my "in-

tended" if she would prefer to be married at home or in the Blue Room at the Capitol, where we could be married in the presence of the governor and other distinguished friends. She replied, that she would take the matter under advisement.

About this time I received an invitation to address the Wolf and Fox Hunters Association, consisting of distinguished hunters from several states, at their annual hunt on the Connie Gibson ranch in the Osage.

I decided that there could be no more proper place for me to be married the second time than surrounded by 500 hard-riding hunters and 300 hounds—under the oak trees in the heart of the Osage Nation.

I did not inform the lady of this scheme but did tell her that on a certain day I was to deliver an address before this association and that she could go along if she so desired—that we would be absent for only one day. Her reply was that she would be glad to go. I advised her that she would meet many noted citizens from Oklahoma and other states and that she should put on her best "bib and tucker."

Accordingly we left in the gray of the crystal morn of a cloudless day, headed for Pawhuska, the capital of the Osage.

About 5 miles west of Nowata, as the sun was rising, one of the most magnificent wolves I have ever seen came out of a ravine; crossed the road about 50 yards in front of us—loping leisurely south.

As the sun shone on his gray coat he presented a beautiful and pleasing object on the landscape. I considered this an omen of good fortune for our enterprise.

Still keeping the lady in blissful ignorance of my diabolical intentions, I parked my car in front of the Osage Agency, stating I was going there to transact some business with the department. In reality, I merely passed through the Agency; came out at the rear and walked to the courthouse nearby. While securing my license, Judge John R. Charlton, pioneer jurist and now a district judge, came upon the scene. Said he: "Senator Graham are you going to be married?" To which I replied: "I am." Then quoth he: "I wish to have the honor of performing the ceremony." I replied: "Judge, I am going to be married at a hunter's meet on the Connie Gibson ranch about 40 miles from this city." He countered: "At what time?" I said that I would begin speaking to the assembly at 3 o'clock; that I would speak for 30 minutes, at the expiration of which time I desired to be married. He replied that he would be standing there looking at me.

All of this time the lady was in ignorance of the fiasco awaiting her—and was sitting with the other ladies in the circle among the large number of hunters present.

I commenced to speak at 3 o'clock; made the best speech I had ever delivered. At the close, Mr. A. M. Young, pioneer banker of Oklahoma City and president of the association, arose and thus addressed the assembly: "Ladies and gentlemen, I have a most delightful announcement to make. Senator Graham, who has just addressed you, will now honor this association by being married."

Judge Charlton approached me and said: "Senator

Cherokee Nation political rally, Sequoyah County.

Bluegrass Festival, McAlester.

Street dance, Nowata.

Serenade at the Sorghum Festival, Wewoka.

Moving to the music, Wewoka.

Dressing for the dance, Claremore.

70

where is your license?" I replied that the license was in my car and proceeded to get it.

As I started, I looked around and the lady had turned white with astonishment at the surprising announcement. Just then Hon. E. T. Newblock and President A. M. Young proceeded to where the lady stood; escorted her to the center, where the crowd broke into a mighty cheer and yelled, "Speech." She was now so embarrassed she could not speak, and as I came up we took our position in front of that noble throng and were married.

We received the congratulations and friendly hand-clasps of all present, after which we drove rapidly away.

We had scarcely left the crowd when my wife said: "That was a mean trick that you played on me, but I will have the rest of my life to get even with you.[68]

A COMPLEX AREA OF GREAT PROMISE

Oklahoma has developed into a complex state of great contrasts. Eastern Oklahoma, which would have become the State of Sequoyah if that convention had realized its goals, mirrors the state's general complexity and contrasts. Modern, progressive cities with highly sophisticated business and industry, cultural organizations, and educational institutions share this beautiful green country with small towns and sleepy hamlets. The majority of its people take genuine pride in the very real gains being made in ethnic and religious understanding within their state in general and in eastern Oklahoma in particular.

Indian people deeply cherish their heritage. Gone are the days when students were punished in schools because they dared speak Native American languages. The Five Nations are again active governmental organizations and the contexts of spirited political activity. They are also vehicles of important social, cultural, and economic activity. The white men who dismantled the Creek Nation could not have foreseen the turn of events in 1976 that revived the House of Warriors and the House of Kings of the Creek Nation and the reestablishment of the ancient Creek tribal towns as the federally recognized governing force operating under the Creek Constitution of 1867. The revival of the Creek Nation is a dramatic example of the widespread renewal of Oklahoma Indian tribal organizations and powers.[69]

Rennard Strickland is correct when he suggests that the most important event for Indian people since statehood is the rebirth of Indian tribal courts in Oklahoma. A jurisdictional and governmental unit known as Indian Country now operates in the arena of federal Indian law and separate from the Oklahoma court structure.[70]

The revitalization of the tribal governmental and judicial units has developed due to extensive and increasingly successful legal battles by individual Indians, Indian organizations, and tribal governments. Federal jurisdiction over Indian political affairs has, as a result, decreased. Litigation has often been long, slow, and disheartening for the state's Indian people. The State of Oklahoma has been slow in recognizing Indian land and water rights.[71]

Given the success Indian tribal units are enjoying in gaining acceptance of their legal rights as dependent nations with special legal relationships to state governments and the federal government, this writer anticipates a negative reaction

Dance break, Tahlequah.

Putting on war paint, Claremore.

Passing on the tradition, Claremore.

Northern style dancing, intertribal powwow, Shawnee.

75

Cornstalk shoot at the Cherokee National Holiday, Tahlequah.

Creeks and Seminoles playing stickball, Seminole.

The bull rider, Wewoka.

Preparing for the State Prison Rodeo, McAlester.

Heading for a fall, State Prison Rodeo, McAlester.

At the corral, Sequoyah County.

Patriotism on display, McAlester.

82

Miller time is rodeo time, Sequoyah County.

Heading for the finish, Ada.

You can lead a mule to water . . . , near Jay.

from some Oklahomans who are ignorant of the history of Indian legal circumstances and relationships. This reactionary attitude sees the Indian nations as simply another set of American ethnic organizations. This attitude must, of course, be opposed by knowledgeable Oklahomans, Indian and non-Indian.

Oklahoma, nonetheless, shows a marked tendency to come to terms with its past as an Indian state. This inclination is shown in the fact that the two state statues in the United States Hall of Fame are Indians, Sequoyah and Will Rogers. The incredible Sac and Fox athlete, Jim Thorpe, joins Sequoyah and Rogers among Charles Banks Wilson's portraits of great Oklahomans at the Oklahoma State Capitol.[72]

Indian political figures, such as Enoch Kelly Haney and Ross Swimmer, are having genuine influence in state and federal governmental affairs. This and other factors give encouragement that eastern Oklahoma is moving into a new period of maturity and self-understanding. This movement of perception gives hope to all those who would understand the State of Sequoyah's past and present, and most of all, the great promise of its future.

Summer silhouette, Tenkiller Reservoir.

Great Raft Race on the Arkansas River, Tulsa.

Last one in's a . . . , Illinois River.

On the way to New Orleans, McClellan-Kerr Arkansas River Navigation System, Sallisaw.

91

The little giant from Little Dixie, Carl Albert, former Speaker of the United States House of Representatives, McAlester.

Community Center, Bartlesville.

Tulsa dawn.

Urban reflections, Tulsa.

Cattle and crude, near Henryetta.

At the auction barn, Dewey.

Farmer-statesman, former United States senator and Oklahoma governor Henry Bellmon, Billings.

August afternoon, near Tahlequah.

Early morning on the Illinois River, Cherokee County.

100

Horses near Sallisaw.

Young Osage, Tahlequah.

NOTES

1. Donald E. Green, *The Creek People* (Phoenix: Indian Tribal Series, 1973), pp. 84-85.

2. Rennard Strickland, *The Indians of Oklahoma* (Norman: University of Oklahoma Press, 1980), p. 34.

3. Grant Foreman, *Indian Removal: The Emigration of the Five Civilized Tribes* (Norman: University of Oklahoma Press, 1932).

4. Strickland, op. cit., p. 3.

5. Arrell Morgan Gibson, "America's Exiles" in *America's Exiles: Indian Colonization in Oklahoma,* Arrell Morgan Gibson, ed. (Oklahoma City: Historical Society, 1976).

6. Richard J. Margolis, "To Live on This Earth," *Foundation News,* Vol. 25, no. 2 (March-April, 1984), p. 25.

7. Muriel H. Wright, *Our Oklahoma* (Guthrie: Cooperative Publishing Company, 1939), p. 86.

8. Arrell Morgan Gibson, *The Oklahoma Story* (Norman: University of Oklahoma Press, 1978), p. 72.

9. Green, op. cit., p. 49.

10. Ibid.

11. Gibson, op. cit., *The Oklahoma Story,* p. 74.

12. Ibid., p. 73.

13. Ibid.

14. Eliot Porter, *Appalachian Wilderness: The Great Smoky Mountains* (New York: Ballantine Books, 1973), p. 60.

15. Gibson, op. cit., *America's Exiles,* p. 5.

16. Ibid., p. 8.

17. Ibid.

18. Ibid.

19. Porter, op. cit.

20. Gibson, op. cit., *The Oklahoma Story,* p. 72.

21. Gibson, op. cit., *America's Exiles,* p. 9.

22. Strickland, op. cit., p. 12.

23. Ibid.

The State of Sequoyah.

24. Angie Debo, *And Still the Waters Run: The Betrayal of the Five Civilized Tribes* (Princeton: Princeton University Press, 1940), p. 5.

25. Ibid., p. 4.

26. Ibid., p. 7.

27. Ibid.

28. Ibid., p. 7.

29. Ibid., p. 9.

30. Green, op. cit., *The Creek People,* p. 56.

31. Ibid., p. 55.

32. Strickland, op. cit., *The Indians in Oklahoma,* pp. 15-16.

33. Wright, op. cit., *Our Oklahoma,* p. 152.

34. Gibson, op. cit., *America's Exiles,* p. 14.

35. Ibid.

36. Edwin C. McReynolds, *Oklahoma: A History of the Sooner State* (Norman: University of Oklahoma Press, 1954), p. 223.

37. Ibid., pp. 225-226.

38. Ibid., p. 227.

39. Wright, op. cit., *Our Oklahoma,* p. 163.

40. Ibid.

41. Ibid., p. 165.

42. Strickland, op. cit., *The Indians in Oklahoma,* p. 33.

43. Ibid., p. 34.

44. Ibid.

45. Wright, op. cit., *Our Oklahoma,* pp. 215-219.

46. Debo, op. cit., *And Still the Waters Run,* pp. 10-12.

47. Ibid., p. 12.

48. Strickland, op. cit., *The Indians of Oklahoma,* p. 44.

49. Debo, op. cit., *And Still the Waters Run,* p. 13.

50. Ibid., p. 14.

51. Ibid., p. 20.

52. Ibid., p. 22.

53. Wright, op. cit., *Our Oklahoma,* p. 237.

54. Strickland, op. cit., *The Indians of Oklahoma,* p. 47.

55. Angie Debo, *The Rise and Fall of the Choctaw Republic* (Norman: University of Oklahoma Press, 1937), p. 286.

56. Edward Everett Dale, "Two Mississippi Valley Frontiers," *Chronicles of Oklahoma,* 26 (Winter 1948-49), p. 382.

57. Strickland, op. cit., *The Indians of Oklahoma,* p. 54.

58. Ibid., p. 53.

59. Cindy Cain, "Park Hill: I Care About It," *Muskogee Phoenix and Times-Democrat,* January 13, 1985, Section A, page 3.

60. Gibson, op. cit., *The Oklahoma Story,* p. 128.

61. Ibid., p. 155.

62. Wright, op. cit., *Our Oklahoma,* p. 307.

63. Keith L. Bryant, Jr., *Alfalfa Bill Murray* (Norman: University of Oklahoma Press, 1968), pp. 22-45.

64. Ibid., p. 215.

65. Andy Morgan, "Oklahoma City Man Has a Case of Political Memento Mania," *The Daily Oklahoman/Times,* January 21, 1985, p. 9.

66. From an interview with Governor Raymond Gary by LaDonna Kramer Gooden, Director of Alumni Affairs, Oklahoma City University, undertaken in November, 1984.

67. This section is based on a January 18, 1985, interview of Henry Bellmon by the author.

68. Gid Graham, *The Dawson-Graham and Allied Families* (Collinsville, Oklahoma: 1983), pp. 117-119.

69. Strickland, op. cit., *The Indians of Oklahoma,* p. 75.

70. Ibid., p. 76.

71. Ibid., p. 79.

72. Ibid., p. 80.

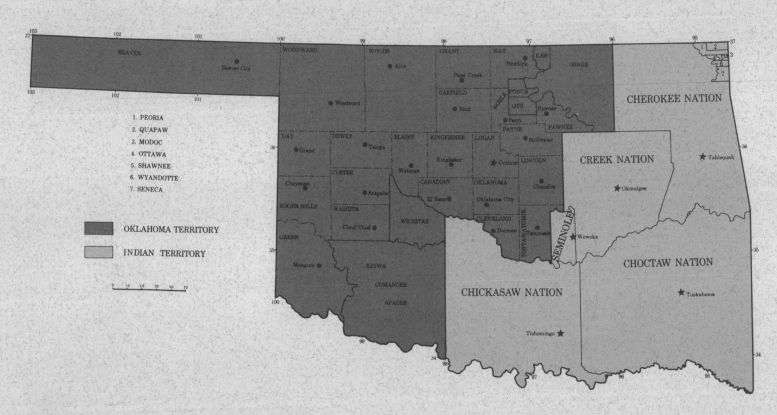

1. PEORIA
2. QUAPAW
3. MODOC
4. OTTAWA
5. SHAWNEE
6. WYANDOTTE
7. SENECA

OKLAHOMA TERRITORY

INDIAN TERRITORY

BEAVER

Beaver City

WOODWARD

Woodward

WOODS

Alva

Pond Creek

GRANT

GARFIELD

Enid

KAY

Newkirk

KAW

OSAGE

PONCA

OTO

Perry

Pawnee

PAWNEE

NOBLE

PAYNE

Stillwater

CHEROKEE NATION

DAY

Grand

DEWEY

Taloga

BLAINE

Watonga

KINGFISHER

Kingfisher

LOGAN

Guthrie

LINCOLN

Chandler

CREEK NATION

Okmulgee

Tahlequah

CUSTER

Cheyenne

Arapaho

CANADIAN

El Reno

OKLAHOMA

Oklahoma City

ROGER MILLS

WASHITA

Cloud Chief

WICHITAS

CLEVELAND

Norman

POTTAWATOMIE

Tecumseh

SEMINOLE

Wewoka

GREER

Mangum

KIOWA

COMANCHE

APACHE

CHICKASAW NATION

Tishomingo

CHOCTAW NATION

Tuskahoma

0 10 20 30 40 50

OKLAHOMA TERRITORY-INDIAN TERRITORY, 1900